Ambition Of A King
Success Secrets

———————————

Jordann Dwayne

This book is dedicated to :

My aunt Barabara who passed away while the was in production . Tay, La'Mya &

Joy Short. Cameron Juniel and his family. My mom Valerie. Normal & Vera Lane.

Karen, Alesia, Lonnie & Leslie Nichols. Grandma & Grandad Adams. Grandma

Jessie & Aunt Lynn. Uncle Richard & Uncle Lee. Uncle Gary & Gary Jr & Aunt

Ana. Robert and Cindy Morales . Loren & Max Guiterrez. Master Chuck &

Instructor Lee. Garret Sanborne & Miss Farinacci . Mr.Hunter. Mrs. Caston.

Justin Holmes and your mom. Brian Mason and family. Eric & "Gucci" Ramirez &

family. Darius & Marcel Jubert. Sunny. Mr'TeamToss & Mrs. Smiley. Howeezy.

Toxic the director and all of Globe Vision Inc. Chris Bacon. Auntie Fiya aka

GawdmamaSauce. Major League Beats. Terry & Toni Raburn. Nicholas

Constantine,Gilbert Stavena & Kameron Porter. Reggie Pettway. Larry 2x.

Dominque Moore. Prophile & Ace Beats. West & Daniel Absher. Dre Barnes. Josh

& Isiah Jackson. Jessika Thrash. Brian Lopez . Joey Reed. Will Whetton . Trawain.

Parker. Frank. Canaris .Ernest St. James Triggo Watson. Lamar. Khayno,Joshua

Bentley and family.Travis Porter. Tony Flame & Nyla.Billy. My entire Media Tech

class & teachers, and my Guitar Center crew for 2013.

& Kristen Raven .

5

*"You have to value the principal of
being wealthy over anything material
in this life, and you will be financially
stable all of your days."*
-Jordannn Dwayne

<u>CHAPER 1</u>
Loose It All To Win

It's simple, growing up with limitations, you acquire a longing for everything that seems out of reach. Race, religion, or sexual preference isn't a factor in deciding how far someone can dream or accomplish. If you take all the moments in life that make your stomach get tense and our heart race accelerate, what do you realize you were most afraid of in your life? Was it actually attempting something or being more scared to start it?

My name Jordan Dwayne, according to the government, is Jordan Dwayne Nichols. Born in '93 to a single mother in Houston, Texas. I've spent the first twenty-six and half years of my life working towards something.

As the proud founder of a custom jewelry company and diamond import business, an art company, and a profitable career as a musician, I've took my curiosity to an extreme level. People always ask me how to be successful or what it is it like being successful and my life answer will always be until I'm in my next life ; I'll let you know when I get there!

There's always a big air quote around the word "success". What do I think makes and made my business more "successful" than the ones that didn't? Taking risks, extensive planning, and taking more time to detail the important little things. Growing up, I wanted to be Michael Jackson when he was in Thriller, a scientist, a soldier and a drummer. My mom wasn't too fond of hip-hop or rap and wanted a more school-based "fail proof" plans for me growing up.

I remember being young and hearing, "Well these bill aren't going to pay themselves," or "How do you think I'm going to pay for all these toys and this house?"   By the time I was seven my aunt and grandparents had come to stay with my mother and I to help out. Being twenty-six now I can honestly say I'm not sure how I would have turned out without them. All three of them were strict. My days of getting in trouble at school with no repercussions were over.

Many groundings. Many spankings. They enrolled me in Tae Kwon Do for discipline and because of

my size . More chores, a stronger
implementation of "yes ma'am, no
ma'am," but when folks ask about
being successful and young I think
back to many lessons and disciplines
of my mom's sister, their mother, and
step-father.

Knowing I didn't want to follow in
line of a "nine to five" after growing
up in a house where that was the norm
meant I had to show, never explain,
more to my folks than myself. The day
that I turned sixteen I had job at this
little pizza place. I was on the drum
line and honestly the only thing that
kept me in school at the time was
music. In those days everyone wasn't
rapping, it wasn't cool to go to the

studio and sell mixtapes but in 2009
you ask anybody at Pearland High
School who rapped and had a future in
it they would of said, " JJ Downz!"
(my old stage name before maturing
into my current name.)
Every penny of my checks would go
towards flyers, CD covers and
pressings, and making sure I was
always best dressed. I went to high
school in a better area of Houston. I
figured all four of my folks helped get
this nice house and that's how we
ended where we did. At a certain age
my mom stopped buying my clothes
and the smaller things when I started
working , which I now truly
appreciate.

In those days me and the
knuckleheads I ran with only cared
about three things: money, music, and
being as fly as possible. So seeing kids
my age parents giving them Corvettes
and Audi's really made me realize
living a bigger life would fall entirely
on myself.

Fast forward twelve years and the
only difference between then and now
is what I know and how far I am
willing to go to build my empire. You
have to lose it all to win. Countless
times in the process of building my
career and business I've been short on
rent, had no food in the refrigerator or
pantry, a negative bank account,

maxed out credit cards, lenders saying too many inquiries, and having nothing to pawn. At a young age age I said I was going to move out, never ask for help, and then send blessings and money to my family at no end. I have asthma and scoliosis so going to the military was out of the question and for the record, yes I was going to cut my hair and lie on the application, but the universe took me a different path.

I realized how much I love structure and discipline when I was younger. Almost as much as the rush of getting in trouble. I yearned for it . I loved watching documentaries on "successful" people, as much as

military movies. I loved seeing people
work towards what they wanted it and
achieving it. I thank Tae-Kwon-Do for
my team building character. I want
everyone around me to win in what
they do as I want to in my endeavor .
All or nothing, or don't start! By any
means risk it all, because before you
win, you lose it all. In that moment
embrace emotional and physical
detachment and you will
witness a higher self. A happier self ,
and a better self.

Anything physically, spiritually
and emotionally achieved in this life is
through setting a goal and seeing it
through . Money is not a reward, but
an equal to your service. Love is not

something that can be purchased, at
least genuine , unconditional love.
Time is more valuable than material.
Apologies are more significant than
the problems that called for them. Life
is too short to dream, and not chase it!
Mean what you say and say exactly
what you mean. Stay true to you. Be
mindful of those around you. When
things look like they couldn't possibly
get any worse.. know they can.
Always work smarter, not harder when
the days are in bright and in your
favor.

<u>Chapter 2</u>
UNDERSTANDING YOUR ENERGY
& OTHER'S

Where I grew up and the generation I grew up in influenced who and what I am today. I don't agree with the term "product of my environment" because if I did , I'm not sure I would be writing this and it would have never reached such an amazing reader. Nevertheless, it did have a huge impact on how I operate my business , deal with stress and loses, and handle my wins. The knuckleheads I grew up with, and you will hear many childhood horror stores in this and the following chapters, were very stuck in their ways. Society teaches young minorities many wrong influences, but by far the biggest conflict that bothered me was my group of "friends" were always teasing me, and I was too "friendly" or outspoken. When it came to selling or promoting anything , I could do it and do it well. I always had the confidence to speak to a stranger, whether it was for business or to get a pretty girl's phone number (even though I often got rejected) .Well   respected among peers, but labeled "too friendly" around my closest friends of the time. It was never meant to be a demeaning term, but it actually made me sit and ponder, every time they would crack a joke and say it. It wouldn't be until going to the BET awards in 2018, that I realized my high school label from my closest friends was actually was one of my strongest qualities. Now, follow me down a side path.

I've met quite a few folks who from the jump wold say, "I love your energy" or, "Man, your energy makes me so comfortable I feel like I've known you for a lifetime! " In 2013, I went vegetarian for about a year on a personal and spiritual journey to cleanse my mid. It was in these days I was learning to focus and protect my energy, or aura , I just didn't know it yet. When you're out in public or with a group of people and things are going good, and all of a sudden somebody

makes a comment , or somebody
lashes out at someone else ,
immediately making everyone feel
awkward or uncomfortable , the
energy in the room just changed.
When you wake up happy, go through
your day & someone comes in contact
with you with a terrible mood or aura,
it instantaneously makes you feel
irritated, upset , anxious and/or a
combination of everything . This is
because you allowed this other
person's energy to bring you down!
When we are unaware of how energy
works and manipulates, we are victim
to those do who understand it or just
have unintentional bad energy .

Your frequency, vibe, and energy must be and has to be protected at all cost. When you stress, your immune system is more at risk for disease and virus. When you are unaware of your energy and how to protect it, you are susceptible to having others energy influence yours!

Choosing who you affiliate yourself with, have a relationship with, and work with all have an effect on your own personal aura. When you are motivated to work out or tackle a task or obligation, take note on how high your vibration of your soul is . Animals picks this up quickly. Ever had a person around who your pet or

even your stomach are not
"vibing"with? You immediately feel
something is off, and so does your
animal companion. This is you
becoming aware of the energy in the
world.

I consider myself wealthy for
many reasons exceeding physical
accumulations. Although I have
asthma, it's mild. Though I don't know
my real father, and at this point don't
care too, I have an amazing family.
Though I don't have any brothers or
sisters, I have 2 cousins Emer and
Alyssa , and an amazing network of
friends, business partners and

associates. Although I haven't accumulated the fortune I have always dreamed of yet, I have many business and revenue ventures that are undoubtedly gaining traction .

One of the biggest lessons I remember growing up is from my grandmother. It was the reason I stayed in trouble until I truly understood what she meant. When I first moved from Missouri City to Pearland at about ten years old, it was the
first time I ever remember seeing so much racial diversity.
"The spots on a cheetah never change" , my grandmother would always say.

"What does that mean grandma?" I
remember asking the first the she told
me that.

I was extremely young at the time ,
"Them kids you run with , they don't
care if you get in trouble , so watch out
for yourself first and always remember
that ." Being a preteen and hearing this
went over my head like the cigarette
smoke my "friends" were always
smoking . Lots of trouble came from
me finding comfort in the wrong type
of friend. There's many ways to say it ,
the lesson doesn't change, only the
story. Protect yourself , and your
energy. Building something larger

than yourself requires understanding of self. I wasn't blessed with perfect health, so the military was out the question. Movies , documentaries , veteran stories and accounts fascinate me from the discipline and fellowship they endured to become a solider. It's sacred and it's certain . The principles in the military don't change , it's their way or the high way.   These very focal points are
how I structured and built Imperial Panache Inc.

I left college (more than once to be specific). The only thing in my life I've ever quit. The only thing is it honestly wasn't a goal of mine, but my family's. My folks always wanted the

traditional background for me.
You know: go to college ,work a 9-5 ,
have a 401k and all that jazz. I respect
that life , but it's just not my style. I'm
not a material driven individual , but if
I want something I'm only going to
buy the best. Once your senses have
been opened to accept and embrace the
energy you give off and who you are
as a person, belittling or shrinking
those ambitions will leave you feeling
empty inside.

Accept, embrace and challenge.
Protect your energy and dreams . For
that is all we truly own in this life
except our perception and happiness.

CHAPTER <u>3</u>
HAPPINESS : CREATE IT OR FIND
IT

It was the last home game my
senior year in high school. It was
already spread to the whole drum line
and band that I was planning a senior
prank. My reasons were of my own
and I had quite a few good ones. My
mom actually even gave me the "OK" ,
as in I wouldn't even get in trouble at
home. During fourth period on the
night of senior night , the band
directors called me in the office and
explained that somebody told them I
was going to mess up the half time
show at the game and do a solo. They
told me I'd be kicked out of band, not
allowed at the banquet, and not
allowed to get my letterman jacket

(long over due anyways). I smiled
and replied "Nah, I won't do
anything ." If you ever run into me ,
ask me my reasons and I feel like my
actions are justified.

I was running with the knuckle
heads growing up, because I thought
we could get money together. It was
all those fights growing up, worth
winning and losing . It was driving to
New York City on expired plates, a
bad tire & no tags, because I had a
meeting with a major label I could not
miss, and my car wasn't going to make
it. Texas to NYC and back to Texas in
thirty-six hours. All because I believed

in something, and stood for it. I
didn't say it was right, by any other
standards or morals, but at that time it
was all or nothing. You will see where
I'm going with this. Oh, and the drum
solo Half time show , it was gnarly.
Got in crazy trouble at school , but it
was worth it. I was happy.

All beings are different in their
own way, but I feel the only thing that
differs me from anyone else is my
desire to get what I need done. I'll do
whatever I need to, or want to, to get
my goal accomplished. Whether it be a
business quota , finding happiness or
making an unforgettable memory. I

could write a book on regrets, but
nobody cares. History only remembers
the biggest risk takers and go-getters.
Achieving my firsy degree black belt
in Tae Kwon Do at a young age,
disciplined me , but only made my
hard headed ways stronger.

The amount of friends and family
I've lost at twenty-six , is enough for a
war veteran. Too many funerals, and
honestly more I couldn't attend would
haunt me for not truly saying good bye.
When you graduate high school it's
rare to keep your same circle of
friends, but in my world... we finish
with who we start with. Granted I've
had falling outs with a select few folks
the majority of my mastermind group
is comprised of childhood friends.

It was a Sunday morning. I woke
up earlier than usual, but like every
morning I started it with music. I
looked at my phone and for the first
time in life a text message had my
stomach in a knot. My heart slowed
and my eyes were unable to
comprehend. Eric Ramirez, God bless
you and the family forever
brother ,was the first person to reach
out to me and tell me one of my
closest friends had just been killed.
Taylor Short. It was July 2014. The
sun was barely waking up itself.   I had
to be at work at 11 a.m. Tay ? My eyes
in the back of my head? My
wing-man ? My brother since
freshman year in high school? I kept
having flashback

the last time I saw his mom. She had me sign this yellow lined half sheet of paper. "You're going to be famous J, " like she always said, but this time she was moving back to her home town in Ohio. "This
is going to be worth millions one day, but this is mine. So just sign it and promise me you won't ever stop following your dreams." I signed and agreed. I'll remember that moment until I close my eyes for the final time.

The following two years were definitely the roughest period of my life. I didn't record much music, and I absolutely got detached from my future goals. I let a lot of terrible

energy back into my life and
manipulate my principles. I became
lazy and distracted. In 2015, I lost
another really close friend, Cameron
Juniel. I met him his freshman year in
drum line camp. I put him in a studio
for the time making beats , and the rest
was history. He was a natural . Two
days after he passed, I founded
Imperial Panache Inc. A small scale
branded t-shirt and hoodie business.

Never did I ever expect things to
be where they are today, even if
dreaming as big as I could in the
impressionable school days. I always
imagined going
on tour and being on MTV. I dreamed
of performing on huge stages. It

sounds like every kids dream, but I
knew, I could handle it and make it
happen. When you understand what
you want, the more everything in life
begins to work in system to achieve
that goal. It's the law of the universe.
Embrace and show gratitude, work
harder and more will gravitate towards
you. People asking me how I ended up
on the inside of the recording industry,
and selling jewelry to some very
important names quite often but the
answer is a lot longer than they're
ready for sometimes. It's this whole
entire book. I think I accepted as a kid
I wouldn't accept a regular life and ran
with that. Any small opportunity to
learn, network, expand, or make a

profit ... I never let it slip by. I treat a
celebrity the same way I treat the old
man with the veteran hat at the gas
station. Respectfully . When you do
that, blessings and opportunities just
seem to fall in your lap. To pass a test,
you study, rest, and don't over think.
To become strong, you exercise , eat
healthy, rest and maintain that routine .
To become successful, you do the
work, set up the pieces on your chest
board , be good to people and
repeat .What you put out will return,
tenfold. What does this have all have
to do with happiness? Well ask
yourself the question a lot of folks are
afraid to answer truthfully or even
ask !

"Am I truly happy? Have I let the world influence me, and it caused me to change or give up on my dreams? Am who I want to be? Am I passing time or fulfilling my purpose? " I like to think as we grow we wake up smarter, almost everyday. The terrible truth in that, is one day way wake up and realize we've made wrong decisions in our journey often treating others not the way the folks who raised us would be proud of. In that moment we can grow, or remain the same. Life isn't about what happens, but how we react to it. Which undoubtedly sets off a domino effect, or a series of events. Now, being conscious of your decisions leaves you with a pretty sensible morale compass.

Not speaking on religion or spiritually, but your mind, body, and soul, knows right from wrong, good company from bad company and bad situations. I don't believe in luck. Only risk. Karma, though, she's a mean one. Do good. Be generous. Speak kindly . Help others. Be honest. Love before labeling. Listening before judging . Understand to adapt.
Being happy, however you may find it, is an energy that shines bright and attracts success! Find joy in building what you know you are manifesting and bringing in your life. Happiness is wealth beyond all.

Do that drum solo. Chase that
dream. To dance. To create. To help.
To lead. To Fight. Believe in yourself
& everything you're doing and watch
your happiness & soul GLOW. Step
into who you were meant to become .

<u>CHAPTER 4</u>
SACRIFICE AND DISCIPLINE ;
WHATEVER IT TAKES

I am going to give you the secret to success. I am going to tell you the biggest industry secret I've spent ten years trying to comprehend. I am going to explain what it takes to make it in any field or profession, what I've paid too much to find out, spent countless hours researching, digging and networking find.

Before I give you the answer to that question though, who am I that you should even believe the answers and what you're reading? I'm just a young soul who has risked everything from freedom to personal relationships to be successful. Maybe we have never met before or maybe we went to school together at a younger age. Maybe we share a passion for personal development that makes our connection, truly outstanding. For you to make it this far In *Ambition of A King : Success Secrets* , and I will explain why I chose this title, we truly are related through soul and consciousness. We are a family through spirit and energy. Total strangers can become family through understanding. That feeling can be so comfortable and inviting, that is why we feel like speaking to certain to people in grocery stores and out in public. Your energy matches the other persons. When you meet someone and you instantly click, that's because you are both on the same frequency. If you happened to read this far in this book, it is a 100% chance that yourself and I would have a pretty meaningful chat over dinner.

So who am I that you should listen to? Someone who is rooting for you to win, no matter the odds. If you weren't sure if you had a supporter or someone who believes in what you're doing, now you do. If you needed that 1% of motivation from someone who knows what it's like to be counted out, this is it. I will leave my contact information in the front of the book, please feel free to email me or engage with me on my personal YouTube channel . Please let me know how to be apart of your support system the way you are with mine!

Finally. The answer that could summarize this whole book into one word sentence.

What is the biggest success secret? We are what we intake , and put back into our universe .

Lets elaborate !

When a car gets a quality oil change that costs more than the cheapest options , then goes and gets some very good fuel that's beating its competitor in quality it rides superior. I wake up some days and forget to eat breakfast because I'm so anxious to start my day and what it brings. The problem with that is you will crash and burn, fast.

You will have to stop what you're doing and recharge your body with substantial food , or your body might just turn against you trying to feed and nourish itself. When you're in physical activities, your coach or instructor makes you get a good meal in before you participate in, no matter what it is. What you put in, you get back.

With success, that is the exact
concept. How can one dive into a field
    with no prior knowledge, research ,
knowledge, tools and blueprint? To
make something bigger than our self
work, we must believe in something
bigger than self. A machine has
working parts, which all work together
to make that object function.
The screw doesn't do the conveyor
belt's job. The bolt doesn't do the
bearing's job. If it did , we would have
a dysfunctional machine! Look at your
success as the exact same concept .
Many working components all doing
their job to help you do yours, which
in result make a profitable, working ,
machine!

Ambition of a King : Success Secrets was the blueprint I used to build Imperial Panache Inc and brother companies, Nichols & Diamonds Imports and Dwayne Cultivated Art co . See a little theme in common? I consider myself a, and THE king in my life and business. The royal power, the commander, the authoritative figure for my future and all will and shall reflect that. Not everyone has the same desires, for all ventures are different. Self confidence and knowing what you will accept as a standard, combined with focused knowledge and the disciple it takes to see a task through, is guaranteed success.

Bring people with amazing energy

and who have good intentions into your <u>power</u> <u>circle</u> (a group of close respected associates, that you consult with). Pay them well. Encourage and appreciate them. Trust them to their job, and together much will be accomplished.

Whatever it takes. Whether its time away from leisure actives or comfort , being successful comes with difficult decisions that impact your future and require a definite and consistent choice of actions. Only oneself must face the decision to make our future better .

I could write a manuscript on discipline alone, but it would only simply drill the same concept. Do what needs to be done, all the time. That's the difference in success and failure, winning and losing , great and mediocre . Take the time to learn your process. Perfect it. Lose yourself in it. Become rebuilt by it. Re-perfect it. Write your goals down and break them down into achievable daily & weekly steps. Attack those goals.

Learn the Value of a one dollar. Spend 20% of what you earn. Save the rest. I'm not a financial advisor so I won't tell you to invest a certain amount, but saving money is

detrimental . Understanding it is no
ones responsibility to put it in position
to win, no matter what the
circumstances are of the many hard
truths to life. I'm not sure if life gets
easier, or we just get stronger. We lose
people. We lose money. In today's
society , it's not too hard to lose your
mind. All those things can
be found again. The hardest thing to
find when lost though, is our own
spirit. Many of the folks in the
dedication list are folks I've known
and personally lost. The strongest tool
in your arsenal of strategies is the
reason you're doing what you're doing

or your purpose. Purpose drives the soldier. Reason drives the champion. Understanding what glues together everything in your success and appreciating the blood, sweat and tears is your reason "Why". Your purpose. However big or small to another individual it may seem, it is your reason. Love it. Let it break you down to the bare, and come back stronger and more determined. Fall in love with the process of beeping, because a destination is only an endpoint.

If you want to be a rock star, study the greats . If you want to become a jeweler, study jewelry. If you want to win, study what it takes.

        Short cuts only cut you short from
the end , because somebody is
working that much harder than you.
Don't cheat yourself. Win and stay in a
winning position. Appreciate and
understand patience and delayed
gratification. Patience is the greatest
virtue of the gods because they have
nothing but time. Delayed gratification
is exactly what is sounds like. Put off
the reward for the work, hustle, or
process, so when the reward comes it
is greater and much more appreciated.
We all have weaknesses to balance our
strengths. We all have unhealthy
habits to balance out our better ones.

The peak of life is minimizing bad practices and habits, cutting off negative people and situations on a day to day basis.

Success is more than a tangible object , of course unless that's all you were searching for. Outcomes and rewards can be multi-faced when you learn to look at things from a higher perspective or a different angle. Become obsessed with learning.

To become great is by realizing that with everything we know, there's a whole world for what we don't. Knowledge is the water to a growing tree. The dirt is the foundation you have set from building a strong network, to perfection of craft. No matter how big the tree gets, it must always have water or it will die. Always be willing to take on the unknown . Listen more than you speak . Give more than you ask. Congratulate more than you criticize.

I have made a list of traits, lessons and mess-ups , and advice that I've learned from running the streets to having a day job, to having legitimate businesses. Spend time each and every day tackling one of the factors and you will witness a change in your life. Success like happiness, is a choice.

1. Time is the most important asset
we have.
2.   The more money you make,
continuously concentrate on
humbling yourself.
3. Money comes and goes.
Unfortunately so do good people.
Appreciate everything.

4. You are responsible for
everything that happens to you and
everything around you.
5. Do it. Regret is worse.
6. Good working habits equal
success . Learn them all.

7. Bad energy blocks creativity.
8. Spend time alone in nature for
clarity.
9. The more physical materials you
acquire, Demand yourself to reduce
attachment to possessions. Love is
more important than any material.

10. Health is wealth. Drink water
and put how you feel at a priority .
11. Don't take life too serious, we
aren't going to make it out alive.
12. Learn to forgive yourself and
others.

13. Travel as much as you can. Learn other people's culture and expand your knowledge on the human race.

14. Let nothing anyone says or thinks about you , affect ANYTHING you are doing.

15. Dream bigger . Get closer to that goal every single day .

16. Helping others makes you sleep
a little better.
17. Stand for something. Die about
it.
18. Focus on today . If tomorrow is
bothering you , write down what is
giving you that anxiety. Open it
tomorrow. Handle it .

19. Create the lifestyle you see in your head. Don't compromise your goals, happiness or dreams. For anyone.
20. Speak what you feel. Communicate respectfully and do not ever feel bad for being you.

History only remembers those who pushed every limit and boundary, and the ones who broke every conventional way of achievement. Something is only impossible until someone figures out how to do it. You have to know you will be successful, before you begin your path or you won't be there. Helping others get in position often results in people helping you when they are settled. The downside to success, I might warn, can be feeling alone or sacrificing temporary happiness for a delayed gratification .

To any and all who have taken
time to read this lesson my deepest
appreciation and extended gratitude go
to you, your family and
everything you are working towards.
Anything it takes. See you at the top.

I would like to thank Mom & Imperial
Panache inc for all believing in
everything I ever walked towards.
Every music industry professional
that's ever worked with me and
believed in me.MTV & BET.
Opportunity Knock Show &
UnderRatedTv. HotboyTurk. Plaquey
Chan. Everybody who bullied &
doubted me in grade school . The very
few people who I called, the very few
times I was in a dark place and you all
helped lift my spirits. My investors.
All of my amazing customers and
fans , I love each and every single one
of you all with all of my heart. I
couldn't do his without each and every
single one of you .

<u>NOTES</u>

My Goals

What are the biggest factors holding myself
back from success?

____

____

____

What do i plan on doing to work around
those goals and stay motivated ?

____

____

____

What is success to me ?

____

____

____

What are my 6 month goals and my plan to achieve them ?

____

____

____

____

What are my one year goals and my plan to
achieve them ?

____

____

____

____

What is my biggest motivation & reason for
to keep me going?

____

____

____

____

Date ___________________

I _____________________________ promise
to self, to make my goals come to true. If i
should fall short , there will be no one to
hold in responsibility but myself. I promise
to succeed !